PIANO · VOCAL · GUITAR

FEMME FATALE

ISBN 978-1-4950-9573-3

HAL•LEONARD®

7777 W. BLUEMOUND RD. P.O. BOX 13819 MILWAUKEE, WI 53213

Visit Hal Leonard Online at
www.halleonard.com

BAD BLOOD

Words and Music by TAYLOR SWIFT,
MAX MARTIN and SHELLBACK

Moderately fast, with a half-time feel

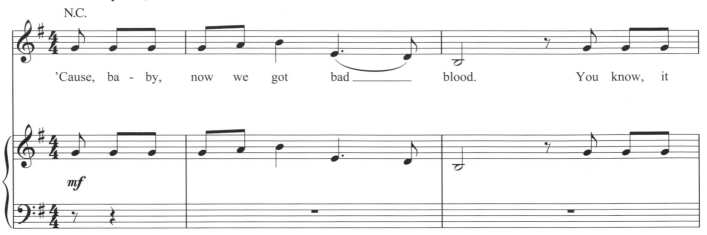

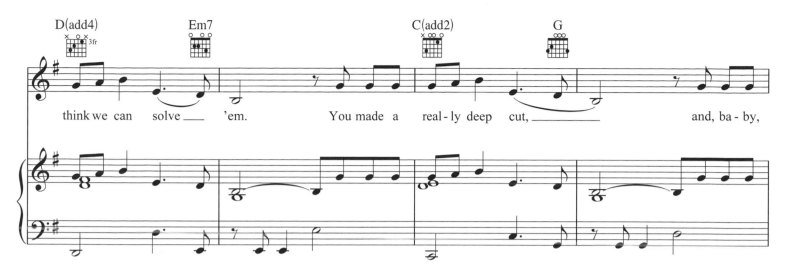

think we can solve ___ 'em. You made a real-ly deep cut, _____ and, ba-by,

now we got bad ___ blood. 'Cause, ba-by, now we got bad _____ blood. Hey!

Additional Lyrics

Rap 1: I can't take it back, look where I'm at
We was on D like DOC, remember that?
My TLC was quite OD, ID my facts
Now POV of you and me, similar Iraq
I don't hate you but I hate to critique, overrate you
These beats of a dark heart, use basslines to replace you
Take time and erase you, love don't hear no more
No I don't fear no more, better yet respect ain't quite sincere no more

Rap 2: Remember when you tried to write me off?
Remember when you thought I'd take a loss?
Don't you remember? You thought that I would need yah
Follow procedure, remember? Oh wait you got amnesia
It was my season for battle wounds, battle scars
Body bumped, bruised
Stabbed in the back; brimstone, fire jumping through
Still, all my life, I got money and power
And you gotta live with the bad blood now

BAD ROMANCE

Words and Music by STEFANI GERMANOTTA
and NADIR KHAYAT

Moderate Techno groove

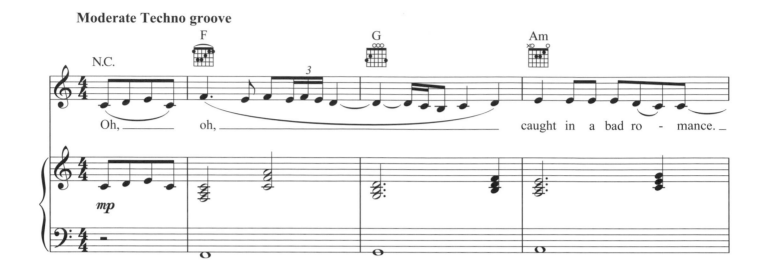

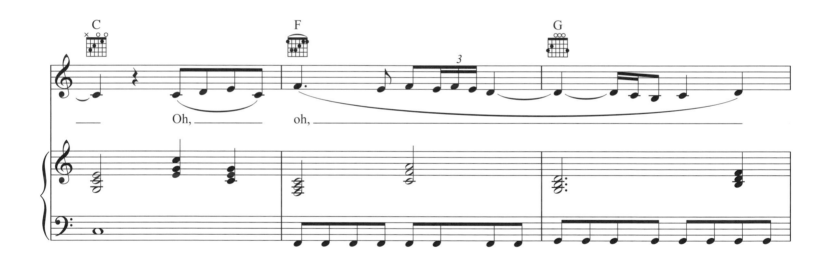

BLACK HEARTED WOMAN

Words and Music by
GREGG ALLMAN

Moderate Rock

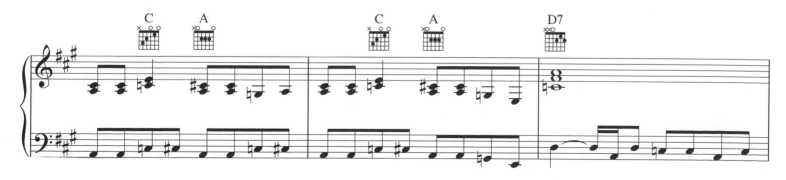

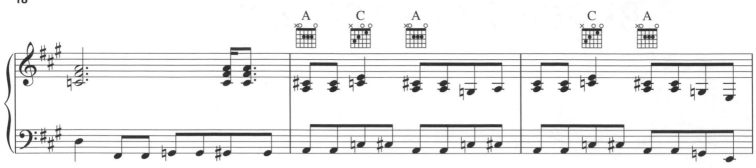

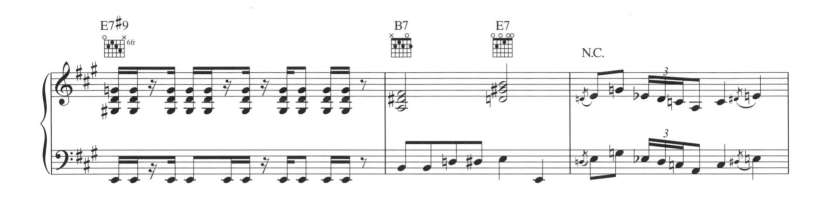

1. Black heart-ed wom-an, _____ can't you see your poor ___ man

2. Black heart-ed wom-an, _____ cheap trou-ble and pain is all ___ you

3. *Instrumental solo*

4., 5. *(See additional lyrics)*

Additional Lyrics

4. Yesterday I was your man,
   Now you don't know my name.
   Yesterday I was your man,
   But now you don't know my name.
   Well, I'm goin' out to find a new way, babe,
   Oh, to get back into your game, yeah, yeah.

5. One of these days,
   I'm gonna catch you with your back-door man.
   Ones of these days, yeah,
   I'm gonna catch you with your back-door man.
   I'll be movin' on down the road, pretty baby,
   Oh, to start all over again, oh yeah.

BLACK MAGIC WOMAN

Words and Music by
PETER GREEN

I got a black mag-ic wom-an. ___

I got a black mag-ic wom-an. ___ Yes, I got a

black mag - ic wom - an she's got me so blind I can't see.

But she's a black mag - ic wom - an and she's

tryin' to make a dev - il out of me.

Don't turn your back on me, ba - by. _____

BLACK WIDOW

Words and Music by AMETHYST KELLY,
TOR HERMANSEN, MIKKEL ERIKSEN,
BENJAMIN LEVIN, KATY PERRY
and SARAH HUDSON

Recorded a half step lower.

gon-na love ya, gon-na love ya, gon-na love ya like a black wid-ow, ba-by.

Rap 1: *(See additional lyrics)*

Play 3 times

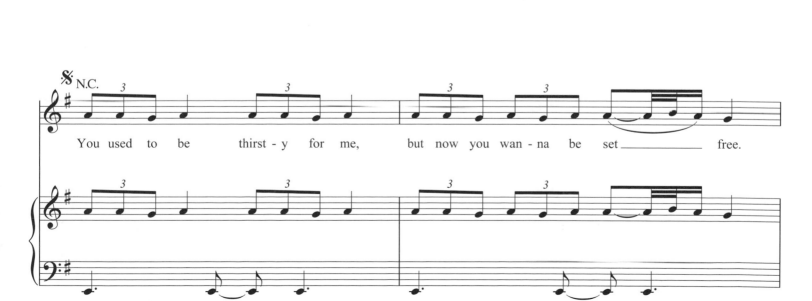

You used to be thirst-y for me, but now you wan-na be set _____ free.

This is the web, web that you weave, so, ba - by, now rest in peace. _____

I'm gon - na love ya un - til you hate me.

And now I'm gon - na show ya what's real - ly cra - zy.

You should-'a known bet - ter than to mess with me, hon - ey.

I'm gon-na love ya. I'm gon-na love ya, gon-na love ya,

gon-na love ya like a black wid-ow, ba-by.

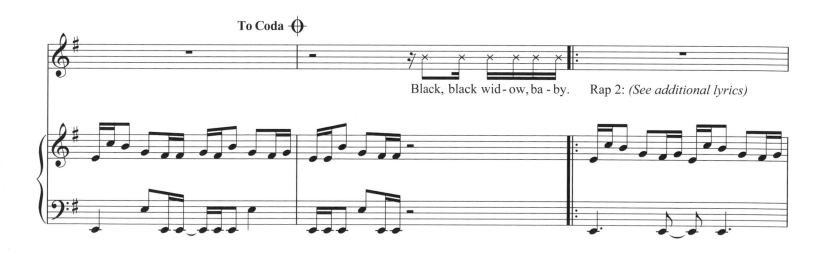

Black, black wid-ow, ba-by. Rap 2: *(See additional lyrics)*

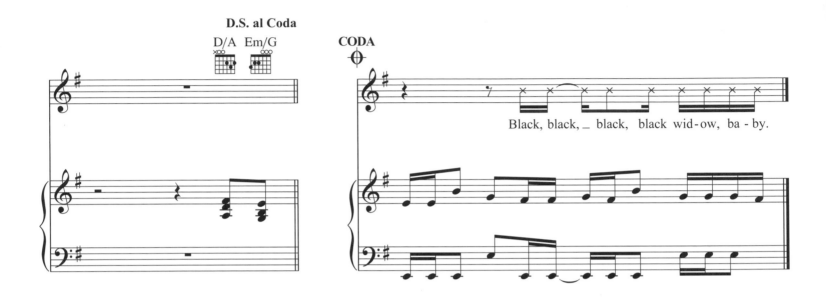

Black, black, _ black, black wid-ow, ba - by.

Additional Lyrics

Rap 1: This twisted cat and mouse game always starts the same.
First, we're both down to play, then somehow you go astray.
We went from nothin' to somethin', liking to loving.
It was us against the world and now we just f**king.
It's like I loved you so much and now I just hate you,
Feeling stupid for all the time that I gave you.
I wanted all or nothing for us, ain't no place in between.
Might, might be me believing what you say that you never mean.
Like it'll last forever, but now forever ain't as long.
If it wasn't for you, I wouldn't be stuck singing this song.
You were different from my last, but now you got it mirrored.
And as it all plays out I see it couldn't be clearer. Now sing:

Rap 2: I'm gonna l-l-l-love you until it hurts.
Just to get you, I'm doing whatever works.
You ain't never met nobody that'll do ya how I do ya.
That'll bring ya to your knees. Praise Jesus, hallelujah!
I'm-a make you beg for it, plead for it, till you feel like you
Breathe for it, till you do any and everything for it.
I want you to fiend for it, wake up and dream for it till it's got you gasping for air
And you lean for it till they have a CAT scan to check on your mind and it's nothin' but me
On it, on it, on it. Now it's me-time, believe that.
If it's yours and you want it, I wouldn't promise I need that.
Till I'm everywhere that you be at, I can't fall back or quit.
'Cause this here a fatal attraction, so I take it all or I don't want sh**.

BLANK SPACE

Words and Music by TAYLOR SWIFT,
MAX MARTIN and SHELLBACK

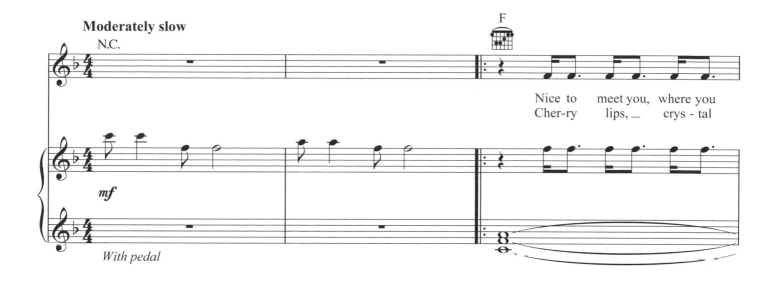

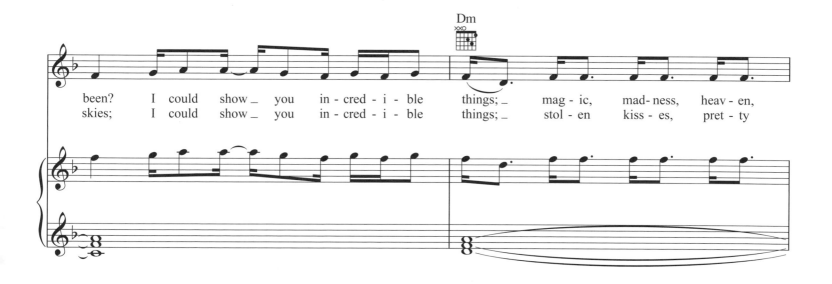

COLD AS ICE

Words and Music by MICK JONES
and LOU GRAMM

Brightly, with a beat

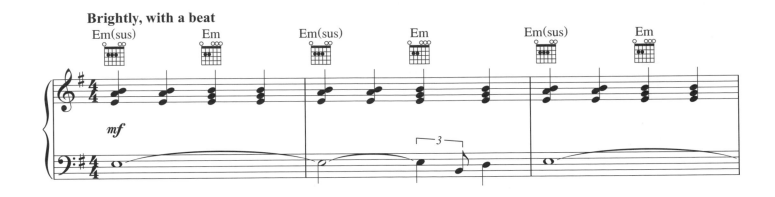

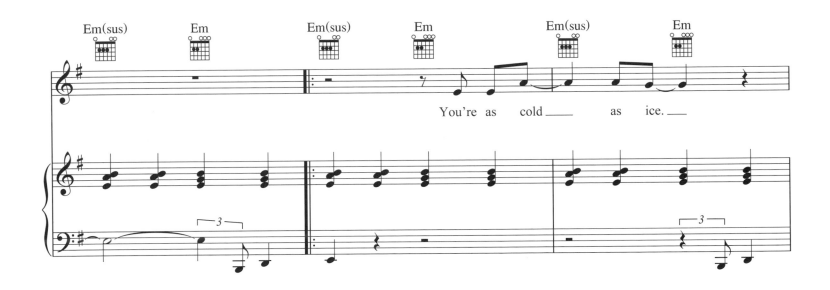

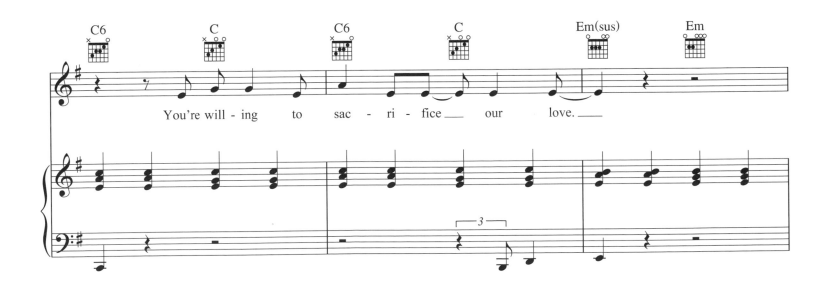

DIRTY DIANA

Words and Music by
MICHAEL JACKSON

CRIMINAL

Words and Music by
FIONA APPLE

I've been a bad, ___ bad ___ girl; ___ I've been care-less with a

DARK HORSE

Words and Music by KATY PERRY,
JORDAN HOUSTON, LUKASZ GOTTWALD,
SARAH HUDSON, MAX MARTIN
and HENRY WALTER

Spoken: "Yeah, you all know what it is."   *"Katy Perry,*

Juicy J,   *Uh huh."*   Let's rage. I

knew you were, _____ you were gon- na come to me. And here you are, _____ but you

Mark my words, _____ this love will make you lev- i - tate _____ like a bird, _____

* *Recorded a half step lower.*

EVIL WOMAN

Words and Music by
JEFF LYNNE

You made a fool of me ___ but them bro-ken dreams ___ have got to end. _____

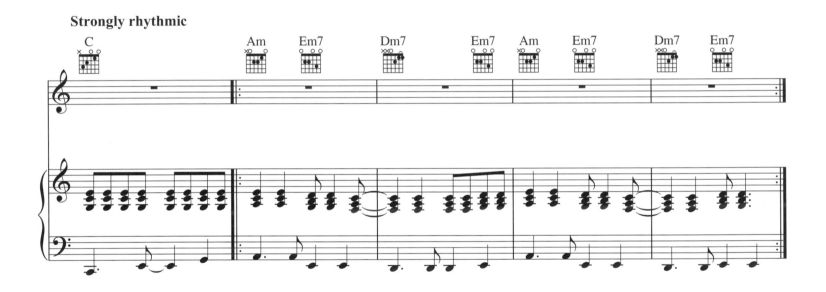

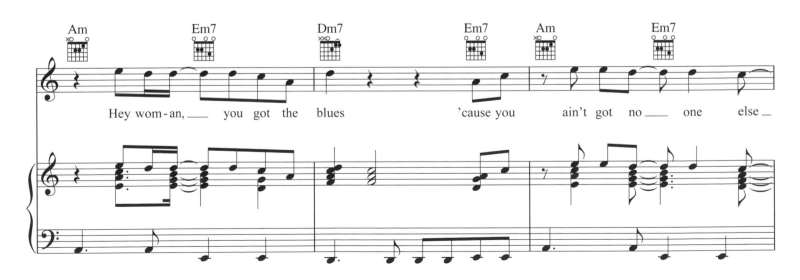

Hey wom-an, ___ you got the blues 'cause you ain't got no ___ one else ___

Repeat and Fade

EX'S & OH'S

Words and Music by TANNER SCHNEIDER
and DAVE BASSETT

FEMME FATALE

Words and Music by
LOU REED

Additional Lyrics

2. You're written in her book.
   You're number 37, have a look.
   She's going to smile to make you frown. What a clown!
   Little boy, she's from the street.
   Before you start, you're already beat.
   She's going to play you for a fool, yes, it's true.
   Chorus

GRENADE

Words and Music by BRUNO MARS,
ARI LEVINE, PHILIP LAWRENCE,
BRODY BROWN, CLAUDE KELLY
and ANDREW WYATT

Moderately fast

Eas-y come, eas-y go; that's just how you live. Oh,

take, take, take it all, but you nev-er give.

Should-'ve known you was trou-ble from the first kiss; had your

INVISIBLE TOUCH

Words and Music by ANTHONY GEORGE BANKS,
PHIL COLLINS and MICHAEL RUTHERFORD

KEEPS GETTIN' BETTER

Words and Music by CHRISTINA AGUILERA
and LINDA PERRY

Step back, gon-na come at you fast, __ I'm driv-ing out of con-trol __ and get-ting
Kiss, kiss, gon-na tell you right now, __ I'll make it sweet on the lips __ as it can

KILLER QUEEN

Words and Music by
FREDDIE MERCURY

D.S. al Coda

ab - so - lute - ly drive you wild, _____ wild.

(She's out to get you.)

She's a

CODA

Rec - om - mend - ed at the price, in - sa - tia - ble an ap - pe - tite,

what a drag. _____

Repeat ad lib. and Fade

LAYLA

Words and Music by ERIC CLAPTON
and JIM GORDON

Medium fast Rock

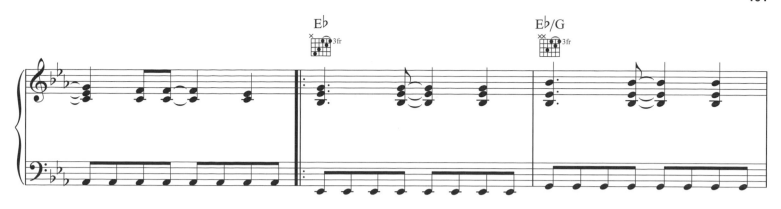

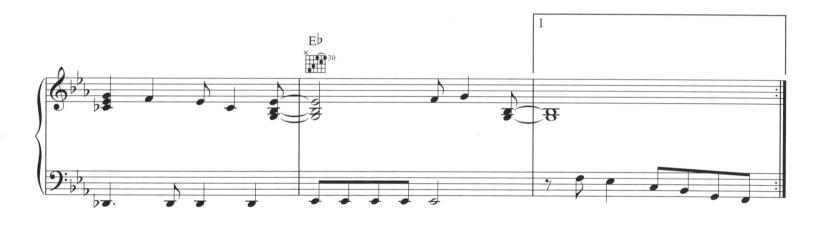

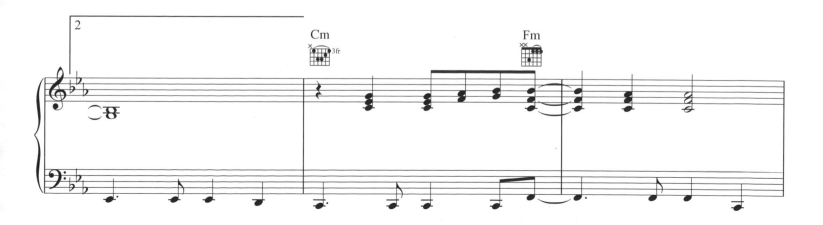

102

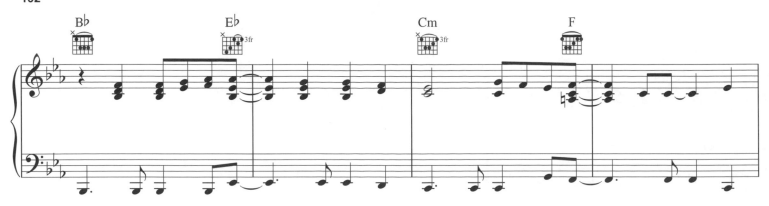

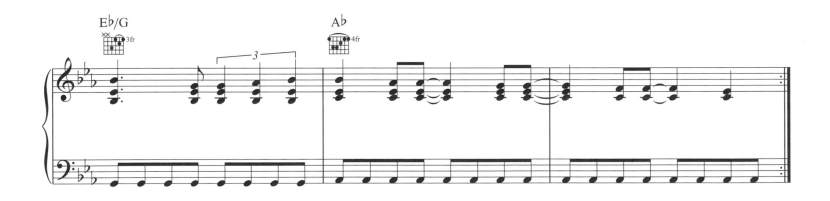

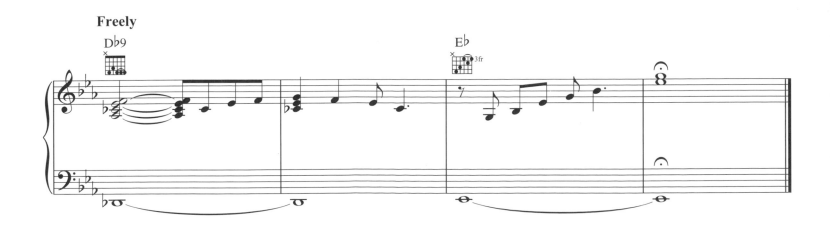

MANEATER

Words and Music by SARA ALLEN,
DARYL HALL and JOHN OATES

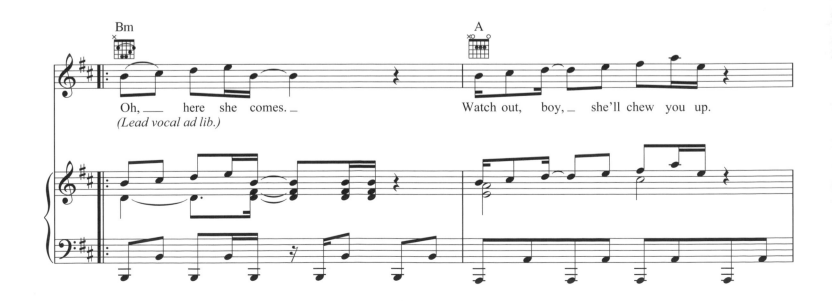

Oh, ___ here she comes. ___
(Lead vocal ad lib.)

Watch out, boy, ___ she'll chew you up.

MAGGIE MAY

Words and Music by ROD STEWART
and MARTIN QUITTENTON

Wake up, Mag-gie, I think I got some-thing to say to you: _ It's

late Sep-tem-ber and I real-ly should be back at school. I

know I keep you a-mused, _ but I feel I'm be-ing used. Oh,

Additional Lyrics

2. You lured me away from home, just to save you from being alone.
You stole my soul, that's a pain I can do without.
All I needed was a friend to lend a guiding hand.
But you turned into a lover, and, mother, what a lover! You wore me out.
All you did was wreck my bed and in the morning kick me in the head.
Oh, Maggie, I couldn't have tried anymore.

3. You lured me away from home 'cause you didn't want to be alone.
You stole my heart, I couldn't leave you if I tried.
I suppose I could collect my books and get back to school,
Or steal my daddy's cue and make a living out of playing pool,
Or find myself a rock and roll band that needs a helpin' hand.
Oh, Maggie, I wish I'd never seen your face. *(To Coda)*

POISON & WINE

Words and Music by JOHN WHITE,
JOY WILLIAMS and CHRIS LINDSEY

Male lead: You on-ly know what I want you to. _____

Female lead: I know ev-'ry-thing you don't

want me to. _____

Male: Your

POISON IVY

Words and Music by JERRY LEIBER
and MIKE STOLLER

She comes on like a rose, but ev-'ry-bod-y knows she'll get you in dutch.
pret-ty as a dai-sy, but look out, man, she's cra-zy. She'll real-ly do you in,

You can look but you bet-ter not touch. Poi - son
if you let her get un-der your skin.

POKER FACE

Words and Music by STEFANI GERMANOTTA
and RedOne

I wan - na hold 'em like they do in Tex - as plays:
I wan - na roll with him, a hard pair we will be.

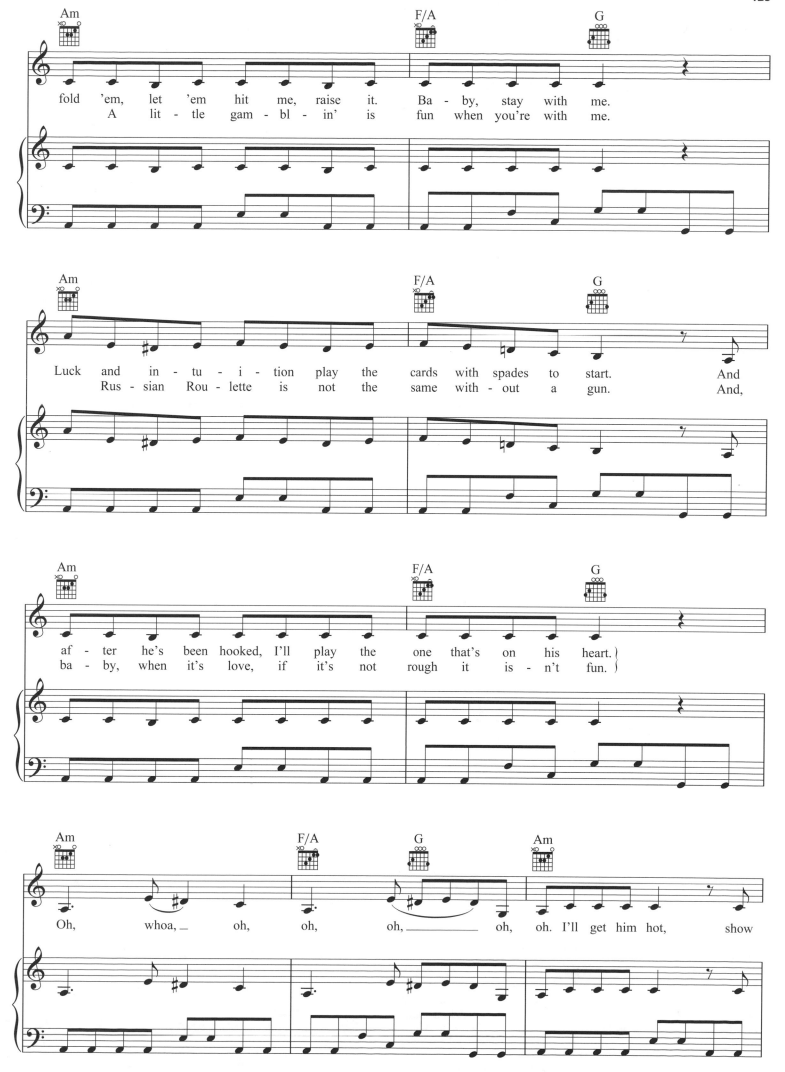

ROLLING IN THE DEEP

Words and Music by ADELE ADKINS
and PAUL EPWORTH

and you played ___ it to the beat. __
nev-er had met me. __ Tears are gon - na fall, __

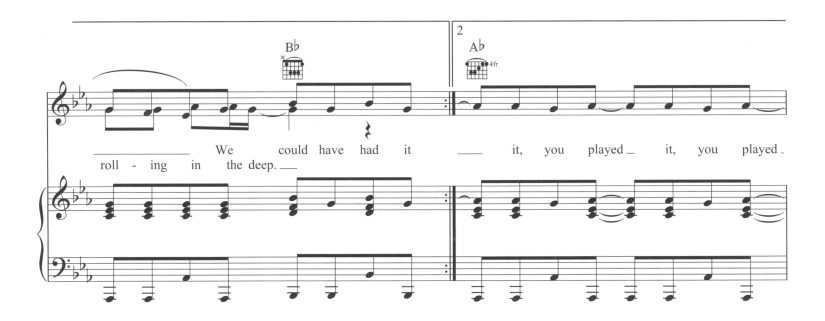

_____ We could have had it __ it, you played _ it, you played _
roll - ing in the deep. __

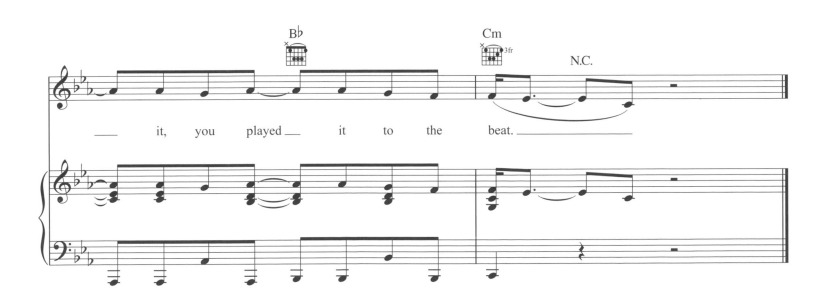

__ it, you played __ it to the beat. _____

UNFAITHFUL

Words and Music by MIKKEL ERIKSEN,
TOR ERIK HERMANSEN and SHAFFER SMITH

Slowly, with feeling

Sto-ry of my life. Search-ing for the right, but it keeps a-void-ing me.

Sor-row in my soul 'cause it seems that wrong real-ly loves my com - pa-ny.

Cm9 Fm6/C Cm9 Fm6/C

He's more than a man and this is more than love. The rea-son that the sky __ is blue. __ The

Ab Ab6 Abmaj7 G5 Gsus G

clouds are roll-in' in be-cause I'm gone a-gain and to him I just can't __ be true. __ And I know that

Ab Bb Cm Bb/D Eb

he knows __ I'm un-faith - ful __ and it kills him __ in-side to know that I am

Ab Bb Ab(add9)

hap - py __ with some oth - er guy. __ I can see him dy-in'.

Fm6
B♭
Cm9
A♭
Whoa, an - y - more.
B♭
Cm9
A♭
I don't wan-na do this an-y-more.
Fm6
B♭
Cm9
A♭
3
I don't wan-na be the rea - son why. And ev-'ry time I walk out the door
B♭
Fm
Cm9
A♭
4fr
I see him die a lit-tle more in-side. And I don't wan-na hurt him an-y-more.

SHE'S ALWAYS A WOMAN

Words and Music by
BILLY JOEL

YOU GIVE LOVE A BAD NAME

Words and Music by JON BON JOVI,
DESMOND CHILD and RICHIE SAMBORA

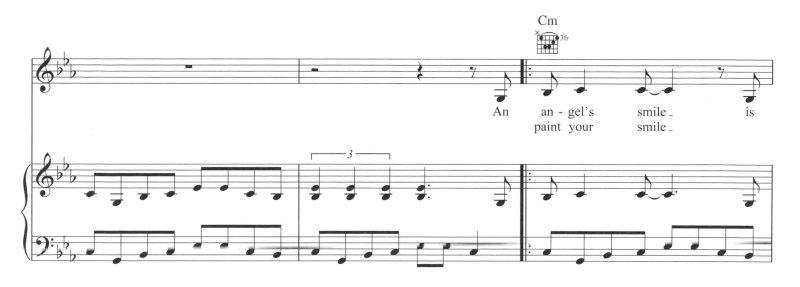

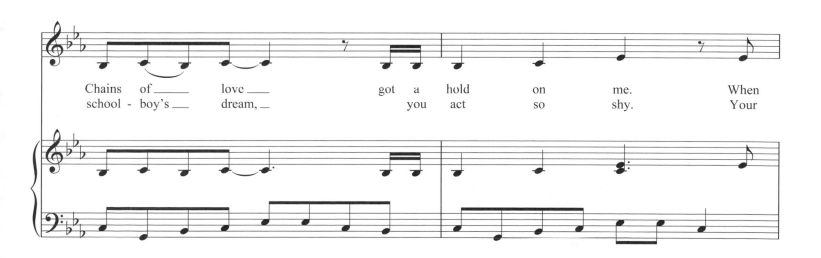